THE POWER OF
POSITIVE
PESSIMISM

PROVERBS FOR OUR TIMES

BY HOWARD KANDEL

ILLUSTRATIONS BY
FRANK PAGE

PRICE/STERN/SLOAN
Publishers, Inc., Los Angeles

Ninth Printing - January, 1976

COPYRIGHT © 1964, 1968, 1969 BY HOWARD KANDEL
PUBLISHED BY PRICE/STERN/SLOAN PUBLISHERS, INC.
410 NORTH LA CIENEGA BOULEVARD, LOS ANGELES, CALIFORNIA 90048
PRINTED IN THE UNITED STATES OF AMERICA ALL RIGHTS RESERVED
ISBN: 0-8431-0041-9

OTHER BOOKS UNDER CONSIDERATION BY THE AUTHOR*

How to Befriend Winners And Influence People

Failure Through Prayer

How To Turn Your Spare Time Into Sleep

Scheme and Grow Rich

How To Make A Fortune In Real Estate Without Getting Caught

Jersey City On $100 A Day

How To Make A Million And Pass It Off As Real Money

Sex And The Simple Girl

Lose Ten Pounds A Week Through Voodoo

Blackmail For Fun

1,000 Free Items And Where To Steal Them

The Nudist Cook Book

*BUT NOT THE PUBLISHER!

NEVER PUT OFF 'TIL TOMORROW WHAT YOU CAN AVOID ALTOGETHER.

Practiss makes perfict.

He who puts his nose to the grindstone is
a bloody fool.

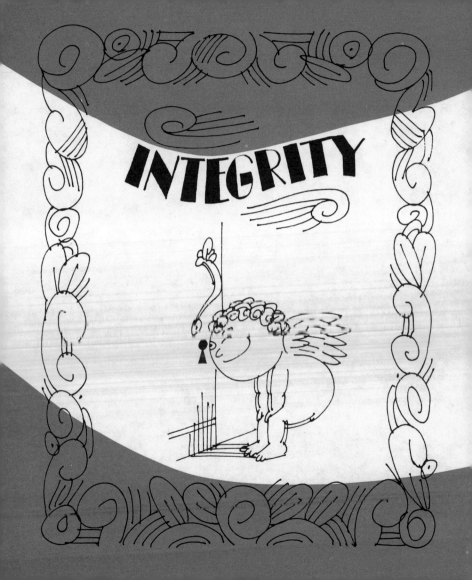

INTEGRITY

HE WHO NEVER PASSES THE BUCK IS A MISER.

If you can keep your head while all about you are losing their's, you're a frigid chick.

He who spurns the wanton wench is a fag.

I DISAGREE WITH WHAT YOU SAY BUT WILL DEFEND TO THE DEATH YOUR RIGHT TO TELL SUCH LIES.

Chaste makes waste.

A little yearning is a dangerous thing.

The devil finds work for idle glands.

FRIENDSHIP

HE WHO ALWAYS FINDS FAULT IN HIS FRIENDS HAS FAULTY FRIENDS.

A friend in need is a pest indeed.

A man's best friend is his dogma.

He who steps on others to reach the top has good balance.

THE PEN IS MIGHTIER THAN THE PENCIL.

Genius is ten percent inspiration and fifty percent capital gains.

He who trains his tongue to quote the learned sages will be known, far and wide, as a smart-ass.

CONFUCIUS SAY TOO MUCH!

All the world loves a four letter word.

In the spring, a fancy young man lightly turns his lover over.

ALL'S FEAR IN LOVE AND WAR.

LOVE IS A MANY GENDERED THING.

Two is company, three is an orgy.

A penny saved is ridiculous.

It's not the money, it's the principal and interest.

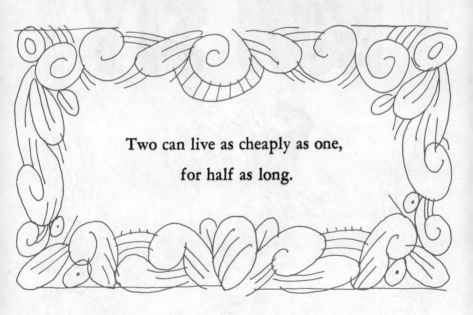

Two can live as cheaply as one,

for half as long.

What ye shall owe so ye shall keep.

He who steals my purse steals cash.

What fools these morals be!

He who always plows a straight furrow is in a rut.

LUST

FAMILIARITY BREEDS.

The bigger they are, the harder they maul.

Let him who is stoned cast the first sin.

YOU CAN'T
JUDGE A
BOOK
BY ITS
AUTHOR.

The early bird catches the early worm.

DISCRETION

A smart man knows on which side his broad is better.

HE WHO USES BAD LANGUAGE
IS AN IGNORANT SCHMUCK.

Expedience is the best teacher.

CHILDREN SHOULD BE OBSCENE
AND NOT HEARD.

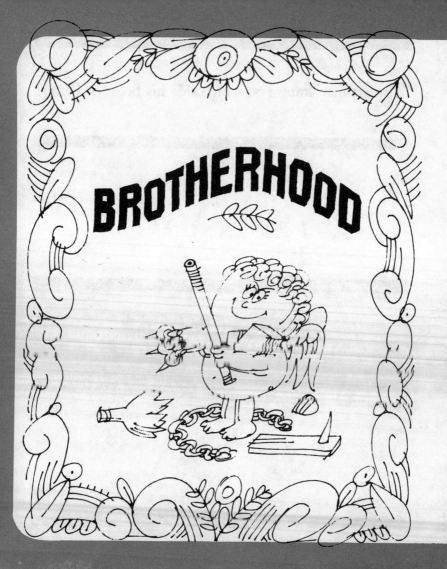

BROTHERHOOD

ASK NOT FOR WHOM THE BELL TOLLS AND YOU WILL PAY ONLY THE STATION-TO-STATION RATE.

Do unto others before they do unto you.

A house divided against itself is a split level.

Love thy neighbor, but make sure her husband is away.

IF YOU CAN'T SAY SOMETHING NICE ABOUT A PERSON, SAY SOMETHING NASTY.

IF YOU CAN'T SAY IT TO HIS FACE, SAY IT BEHIND HIS BACK.

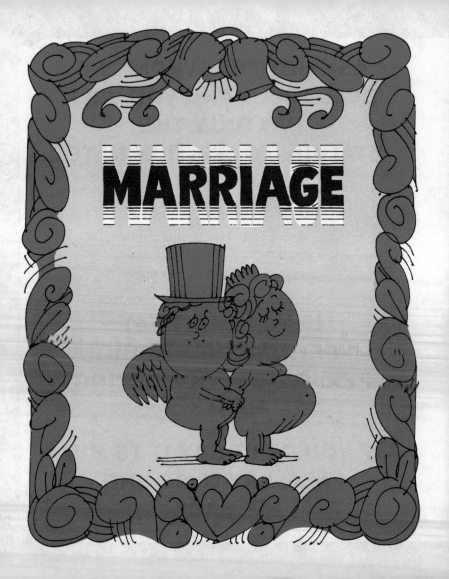

MARRIAGE

It takes two to tangle.

A man must do something
to relieve the monogamy.

'Tis better to have loved and lust.

A man's house is his hassle.

Give a man enough hope and he'll hang himself.

WHERE THERE'S A WILL, THERE'S AN INHERITANCE TAX.

He who hesitates is constipated.

WEALTH

Bank-o-Plenty
CREDIT CARD
43120-6978824

He who inherits riches shall never know the joy of toiling endlessly for his daily bread.

Money is the root of all evil and a man needs roots.

The best things in life are for a fee.

DAMN THE TORPEDOES! FULL SPEED AHEAD!

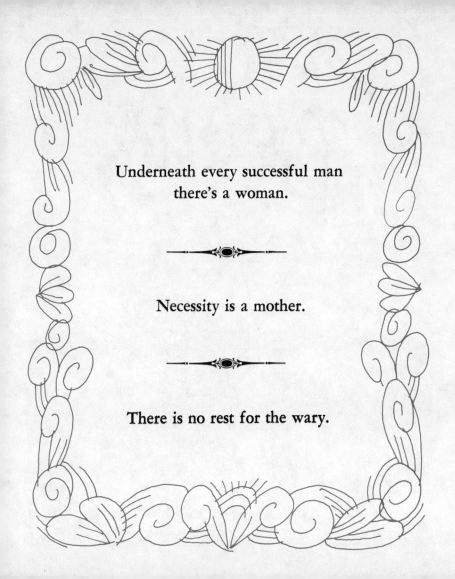

Underneath every successful man
there's a woman.

Necessity is a mother.

There is no rest for the wary.

BENEATH A ROUGH
EXTERIOR OFTEN
BEATS A HARLOT
OF GOLD.

TURN THEM UPSIDE
DOWN AND THEY
ALL LIKE A LOOK.

All's well that ends well and vice-versa.

He who is flogged by fate and laughs the louder
is a masochist.

You can fool some of the people all of the time,
and all of the people some of the time, but you can
make a fool of yourself anytime.

ALWAYS BE SINCERE, EVEN WHEN YOU DON'T MEAN IT.

An honest man's word is as good as his blonde's.

Squaw who speaks with forked tongue can
teach young brave many new tricks.

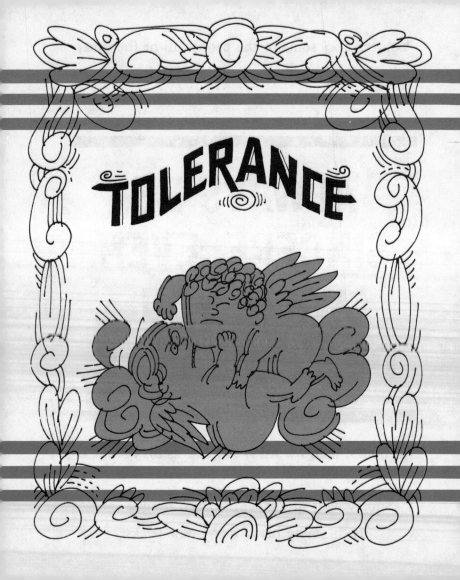

Let us remember that ours is a nation
of lawyers and order.

Everyone has a right to my own opinion.

People who live in stone houses shouldn't
throw glasses.

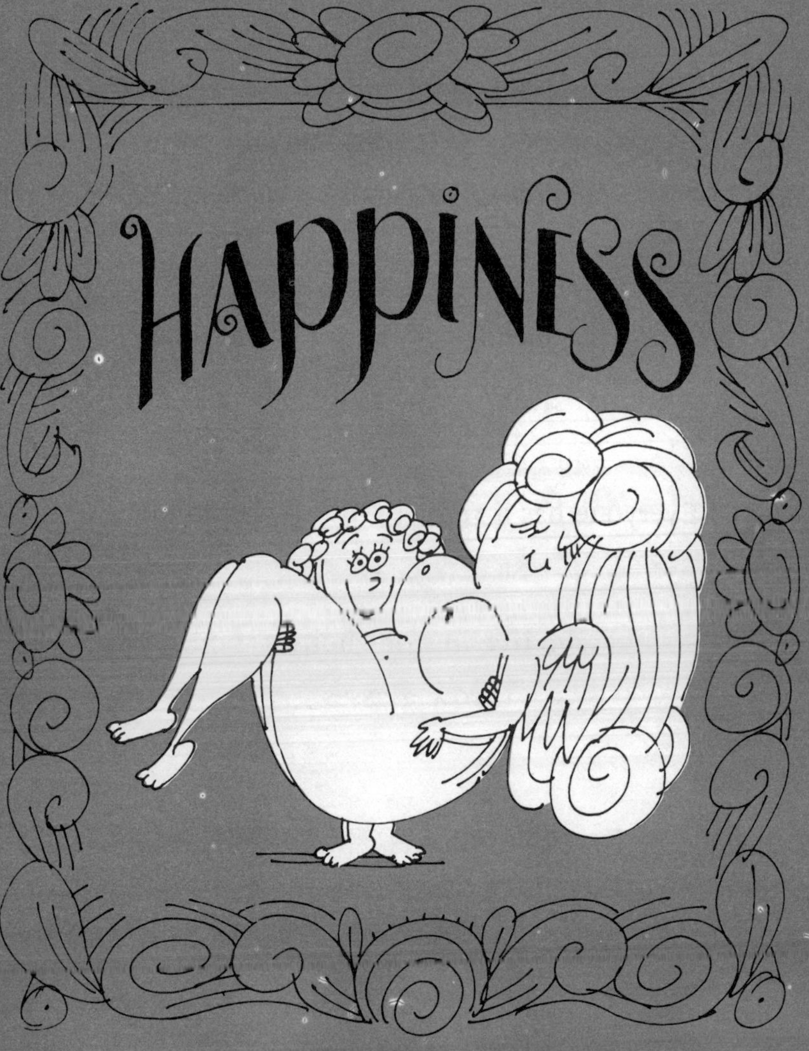
HAPPINESS